Tadpole Books are published by Jump!, 5357 Penn Avenue South, Minneapolis, MN 55419, www.jumplibrary.com

Copyright ©2019 Jump. International copyright reserved in all countries. No part of this book may be reproduced in any form without written permission from the publisher.

Editor: Jenna Trnka **Designer:** Anna Peterson **Translator:** Annette Granat

Photo Credits: Eric Isselee/Shutterstock, cover, 1, 6–7, 16bm; Anup Shah/Age Fotostock, 2–3; dean bertoncelj/Shutterstock, 4–5, 16tm; Nilesh Rathod/iStock, 8–9, 16bl; Guido Bissattini/Shutterstock, 10–11, 16tr; Pranav Chadha/Shutterstock, 12–13, 16tl; Russell Burden/Getty, 14–15, 16br.

Library of Congress Cataloging-in-Publication Data
Names: Nilsen, Genevieve, author.
Title: Los cachorros del leon / por Genevieve Nilsen.
Other titles: Lion cubs. Spanish
Description: Tadpole edition. | Minneapolis, MN: Jump!, Inc., (2019) | Series: Animales bebés de los safaris |
Audience: Age 3–6. | Includes index.
Identifiers: LCCN 2018037635 (print) | LCCN 2018038687 (ebook) | ISBN 9781641285469 (ebook) | ISBN 9781641285452 (hardcover : alk. paper) | ISBN 9781641286824 (pbk.)
Subjects: LCSH: Lion—Infancy—Juvenile literature.
Classification: LCC QL737.C23 (ebook) | LCC QL737.C23 N5618 2019 (print) | DDC 599.75713/92—dc23
LC record available at https://lccn.loc.gov/2018037635

ANIMALES BEBÉS DE LOS SAFARIS

LOS CACHORROS DEL LEÓN

por Genevieve Nilsen

TABLA DE CONTENIDO

Los cachorros del león 2

Repaso de palabras 16

Índice 16

LOS CACHORROS DEL LEÓN

¿Qué son estos bebés?

Tienen manchas.

Aprenden.